★American Girl®

Inspiring Stories From the Past

INSIGHT
KIDS

SAN RAFAEL · LOS ANGELES · LONDON

MEET KAYA

NAME: Kaya

NICKNAMES: Magpie

HOME: Salmon River Country
(Present-day Idaho)

HAIR: Black   EYES: Brown

DREAMS OF: Becoming a courageous
leader of the Nez Perce tribe

YEAR: 1764

Kaya races her horse, Steps High, against Fox Tail and Raven.
Steps High runs like the wind and almost bucks Kaya off her back!

Kaya and her sister Speaking Rain are taken by raiders.
They are forced to work in the raiders' camp until Kaya makes her escape.

Kaya and her sister Speaking Rain are taken by raiders.
They are forced to work in the raiders' camp until Kaya makes her escape.

4

Kaya races her horse, Steps High, against Fox Tail and Raven.
Steps High runs like the wind and almost bucks Kaya off her back!

Kaya befriends a captive named Two Hawks, and they escape together.
They journey through the dangerous forest, and Kaya is reunited with her tribe.

KAYA'S WORLD WORD SEARCH

Find and circle the words listed below by searching up, down, forward, backward, and diagonally.

```
F W H Q Y T D F E Y
T R I V E R R I H Y
L U K M L M P V K J
O I D X L G U M A O
K L J U A I R T Y N
T A N M V F Y Y A N
S R E D I A R L E O
N Q H X L B D Z Q T
V O W O L U P T D X
Z R M D R E Z W B G
B L V L R S N O Z K
N M R C A C E F L B
P H E W C S V T K C
```

KAYA
NEZ PERCE
SALMON

RIVER
VALLEY
HORSE

MAGPIE
RAIDERS

Answers in the back of the book.

ON THE MAP

When Kaya escapes from the enemy tribe, she uses the stars
and familiar landmarks to find her way home. Use the space
below to draw a map of your neighborhood. Include landmarks
that a friend could use to find a path to your home.

MEET FELICITY

NAME: Felicity Merriman

NICKNAME: Lissie

HOME: Williamsburg, Virginia

HAIR: Red

EYES: Green

PERSONALITY: Felicity is fiercely loyal, independent, and spirited

YEAR: 1774

Felicity loves riding horses far more than quiet, ladylike activities such as stitchery.

Felicity and her siblings visit their grandfather at his plantation.

Felicity is supposed to politely serve tea. Instead, she and Annabelle argue about politics!

FELICITY'S COLONIAL WORD SEARCH

Find and circle the words listed below by searching up, down, forward, backward, and diagonally.

```
P  L  F  R  X  O  Y  A  W  L
T  C  Q  C  Z  L  I  B  I  P
S  O  K  N  R  N  R  X  L  K
B  L  O  Z  I  E  O  A  L  U
T  O  E  G  E  W  N  I  I  I
K  N  R  C  N  T  O  J  A  E
L  I  H  C  A  K  L  M  M  T
V  E  P  T  J  Q  C  D  S  A
S  S  I  N  S  H  S  S  B  L
Y  O  R  K  T  O  W  N  U  O
N  R  A  T  I  U  G  T  R  C
R  C  B  M  H  D  N  O  G  O
T  A  O  C  I  T  T  E  P  H
F  K  B  F  S  U  O  E  Q  C
```

WILLIAMSBURG   COLONIES   PETTICOAT
VIRGINIA   PLANTATION   GUITAR
YORKTOWN   BREECHES   CHOCOLATE

Answers in the back of the book.

NOT IN THIS PICTURE

This picture might look like the same image of Felicity's tea with friends, but it's not. Several items are not in the picture. Can you pick out the items that are missing in the scene?

Go back and take a look at the picture on page 11. Stare at it for five seconds to commit it to memory. Then come back to this page to test your memory.

Answers in the back of the book.

MEET JOSEFINA

NAME: María Josefina Montoya

HOME: New Mexico

HAIR: Dark Brown

EYES: Brown

DREAMS OF: Becoming a *curandera*, or healer

YEAR: 1824

Josefina and her sisters are thrilled to meet
their aunt, Tía Dolores, for the first time.

Josefina loves her mother's handmade doll, Niña. Her sister Clara
sewed a new dress for Niña and gave her to Josefina for Christmas.

Papá plays his violin for the family for the first time since Mamá passed away.

MEMORY BOOK

Josefina's Tia Dolores made a memory book and filled it with her favorite memories from when she was a child. Fill in the blanks below to make your own memory journal.

Name:

_____

Age:

_____

Nickname:

_____

Favorite book:

_____

Favorite movie:

_____

Favorite holiday:

_____

Favorite food:

_____

Favorite American Girl:

_____

Best friend:

_____

Best class in school:

_____

Use three words to describe yourself:

_____

What do you want to be when you grow up?

_____

Do you have a pet? If so, what's their name?

_____

What has been your best birthday and why?

_____

Favorite thing to do on a sunny day:

_____

Favorite thing to do on a rainy day:

_____

JOSEFINA'S WORLD

Place the words in the crossword puzzle below
that match the information about Josefina.

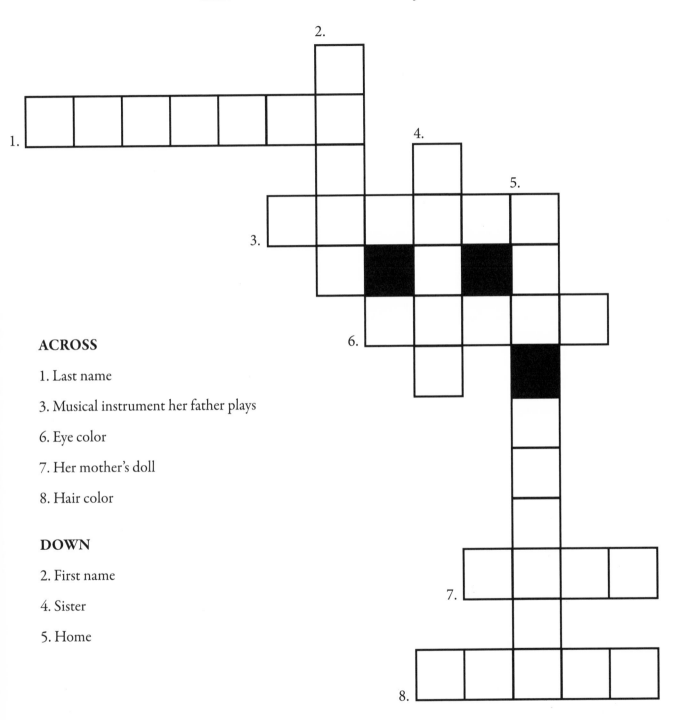

ACROSS

1. Last name

3. Musical instrument her father plays

6. Eye color

7. Her mother's doll

8. Hair color

DOWN

2. First name

4. Sister

5. Home

MEET KIRSTEN

NAME: Kirsten Larson

HOME: Minnesota

HAIR: Blonde

EYES: Light Blue

PERSONALITY: Brave and steadfast

YEAR: 1854

Kirsten's teacher, Miss Winston, shows her a ship in a bottle that looks
just like the ship Kirsten's family sailed on from Sweden to America.

Kirsten, her little brother, Peter, and Peter's dog, Caro, find a baby bear cub.
When the mama bear emerges from the forest, Kirsten, Peter, and Caro flee to safety.

Kirsten goes trapping in the forest with her
brother Lars and his friend John Stewart.

AT HOME WITH KIRSTEN

Kirsten's family were pioneers, and they lived in a log cabin.
What kind of house would you like to live in? Draw it here.

DRAW KIRSTEN

Using the grid as a guide, draw Kirsten below.

MEET ADDY

NAME: Aduke Walker

NICKNAME: Addy

HOME: Philadelphia, Pennsylvania

HAIR: Dark Brown

EYES: Brown

DREAMS OF: Reuniting with her family in freedom

YEAR: 1864

Addy and Momma escape slavery disguised as a boy and a man. After many dangers, they arrive at Miss Caroline's, their first stop on the Underground Railroad.

Addy goes to school for the first time in Philadelphia, where she learns
how to read and write. She then teaches Momma her lessons after school.

Poppa reunites with the family in Philadelphia. They plant a
garden to raise funds for a trip to find the rest of Addy's family.

SPELLING MATCH

Addy won the spelling match in her class, which included the following words. Can you complete the words from her spelling match by filling in the missing letters from the jumble of letters at the top? (Cross out each letter when you use it to remove it from the jumble.)

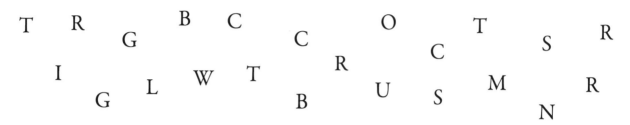

1. CA __ __ I A __ E
(A mode of transportation)

2. __ U __ T O __
(Something sewn on clothes)

3. __ O __ ORR __ __
(The next day)

4. AC __ O __ N __
(A record of money spent and received)

5. __ R __ D __ E
(A structure spanning a waterway or road)

6. S __ I __ __ O __ S
(A tool to cut paper or cloth)

7. P __ IN __ IP __ E
(A moral guide)

NOT IN THIS PICTURE

This picture might look like the same image of Addy in her classroom, but it's not. Several items are missing. Can you pick out the items that are missing in the scene?

Go back and take a look at the picture on page 28. Stare at it for five seconds to commit it to memory. Then come back to this page to test your memory.

MEET SAMANTHA

NAME: Samantha Parkington

NICKNAME: Sam

HOME: Mount Bedford, New York

HAIR: Dark Brown   EYES: Brown

DREAMS OF: Having a family of her own

YEAR: 1904

32

Samantha falls out of an oak tree in Grandmary's backyard
when her neighbor Eddie Ryland surprises her.

Samantha's friend Nellie had never gone to school before,
so Samantha tutors her in reading and writing after school.

After seeing children working in factories and the daily dangers they face,
Samantha gives a speech about child labor at her school's speaking contest.

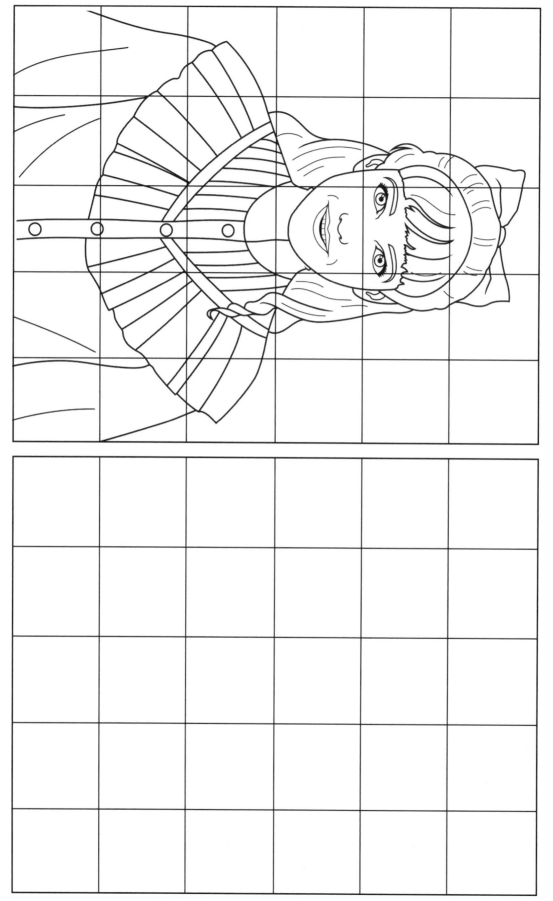

DRAW SAMANTHA

Using the grid as a guide, draw Samantha below.

SAMANTHA'S WORLD

Place the words in the crossword puzzle below
that match the information about Samantha.

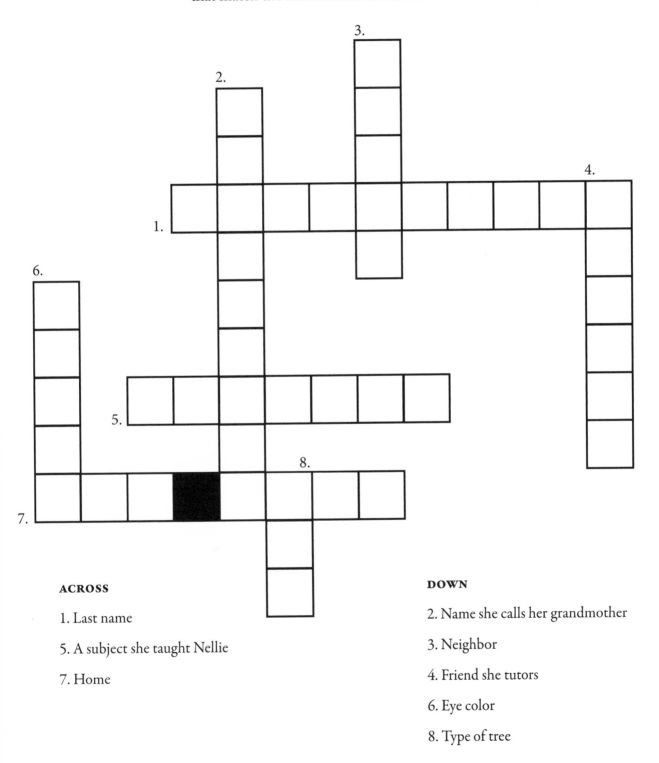

ACROSS

1. Last name

5. A subject she taught Nellie

7. Home

DOWN

2. Name she calls her grandmother

3. Neighbor

4. Friend she tutors

6. Eye color

8. Type of tree

Answer Key: 1. Parkington; 2. Grandmary; 3. Eddie; 4. Nellie; 5. Reading; 6. Brown; 7. New York; 8. Oak.

MEET REBECCA

NAME: Rebecca Rubin

NICKNAME: Beckie

HOME: Lower East Side of New York City

HAIR: Brown   EYES: Hazel

DREAMS OF: Being an actress

YEAR: 1914

At Sabbath dinner, Rebecca pantomimes a story that
her cousin Max—a real actor!—tells by candlelight.

Rebecca visits a movie set and meets the beautiful star, Lily Armstrong.
And her dream comes true when she gets a surprise role in the movie.

After seeing the horrible conditions at the factory where her uncle and cousin work, Rebecca joins a protest and even makes a speech at a Labor Day picnic.

REBECCA'S WORLD WORD SEARCH

Find and circle the words listed below by searching up,
down, forward, backward, and diagonally.

ACTOR   FACTORY   PICNIC

CANDLE   HANUKKAH   SABBATH

DINNER   MOVIE   TEACHER

```
T C C J S C X H R T N
E C Z I A A A Y O U V
A C S N N K B E T L M
C R D O K C I B C J N
H L L U D V I G A G G
E S N V O U D P Y T S
R A O M R X I S P G H
H F A C T O R Y A J N
Z R J C X G A I V V K
D V U Q E T I P Y V A
S R E N N I D C Z Y G
```

Answers in the back of the book.

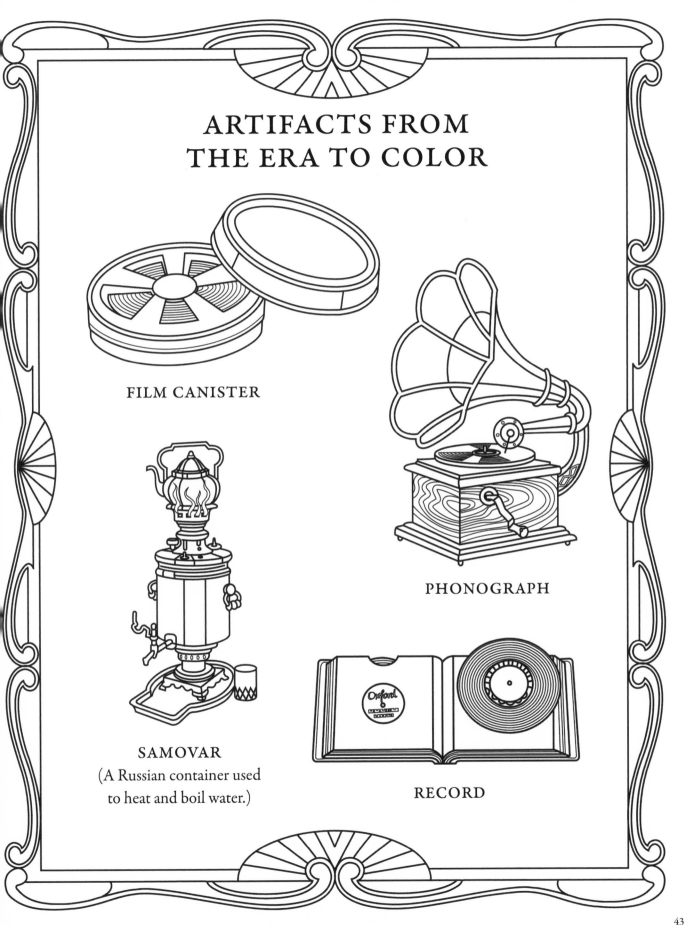

ARTIFACTS FROM
THE ERA TO COLOR

FILM CANISTER

PHONOGRAPH

SAMOVAR
(A Russian container used
to heat and boil water.)

RECORD

MEET KIT

NAME: Margaret Mildred Kittredge

NICKNAME: Kit

HOME: Cincinnati, Ohio

HAIR: Blonde

DREAMS OF: Becoming a reporter

YEAR: 1934

EYES: Blue

Kit types up a newspaper of her family's latest
news with her friends, Ruthie and Stirling.

Kit visits a hobo camp and learns about the
struggles of hoboes during the Great Depression.

Kit and Stirling hop a freight train with their friend
Will Shepherd, a hobo. But they get caught in the act!

FOLLOW THE TRACKS

Kit's hobo friends ride freight trains to get from place to place. Follow the train tracks below to get Kit back home. Which track is the right path?

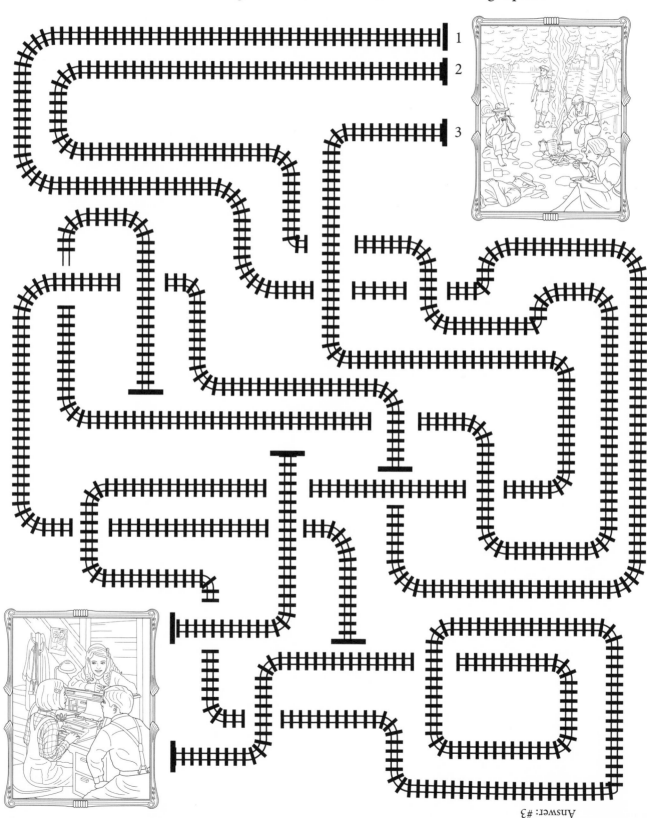

READ ALL ABOUT IT!

Newspapers use headlines to grab readers' attention. Sometimes, the crazier the headline is, the more readers want to buy the paper. Write headlines for the pictures below. Make them as serious or as wild as you want them to be. The first one is already done for you.

Local Girl Has Big Adventure

MEET NANEA

NAME: Nanea Mitchell

HOME: Honolulu, Hawaii

HAIR: Brown

EYES: Hazel

DREAMS OF: Becoming a teacher

YEAR: 1941

Nanea sees Japanese fighter planes overhead.
The planes attack the naval base at Pearl Harbor.

An Army lieutenant asks for Nanea's dog, Mele,
to serve in the Dogs for Defense program.

Nanea performs a hula dance, and Mele gets in on the act too!

NANEA'S WORLD

Place the words in the crossword puzzle below
that match the information about Nanea.

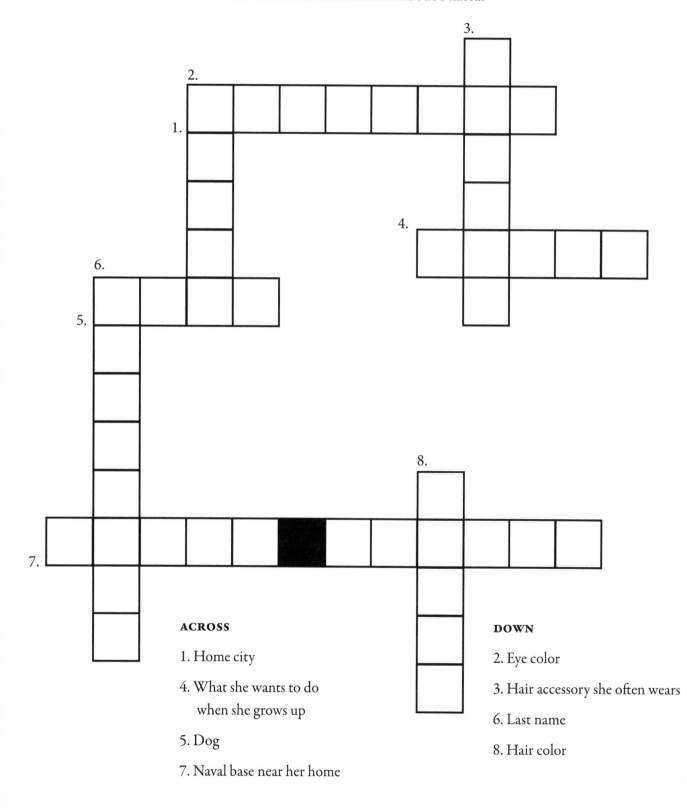

ACROSS

1. Home city

4. What she wants to do
   when she grows up

5. Dog

7. Naval base near her home

DOWN

2. Eye color

3. Hair accessory she often wears

6. Last name

8. Hair color

Answer Key: 1. Honolulu, 2. Hazel; 3. Flower; 4. Teach; 5. Mele; 6. Mitchell; 7. Pearl Harbor; 8. Brown

MATCHING MELE

When Mele goes missing, Nanea and her friends draw pictures of her to make a lost poster. Mele looks a little different in each of the pictures. The same is true about the pictures of Mele below. Draw a line from the picture of Mele in Column A that matches the picture of Mele in Column B.

COLUMN A   COLUMN B

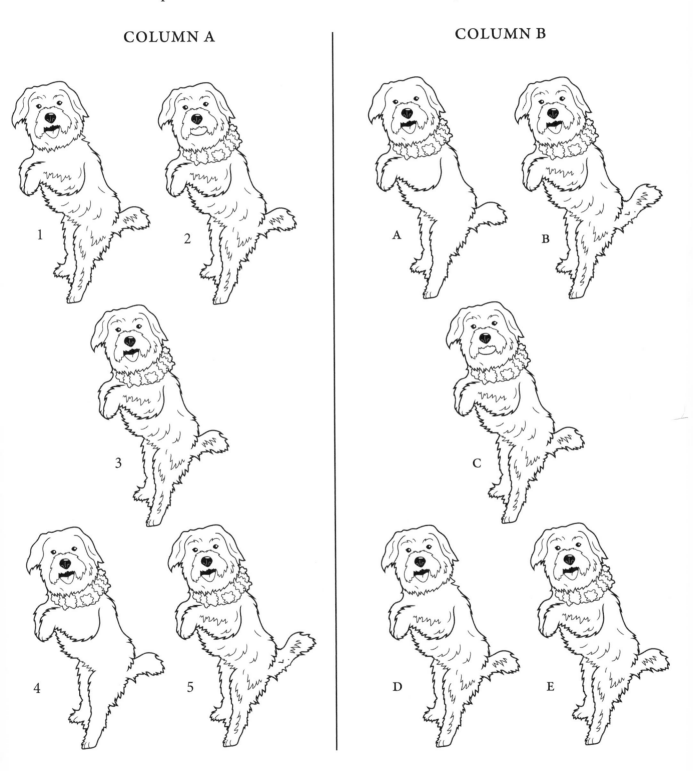

MEET MOLLY

NAME: Molly McIntire

HOME: Jefferson, Illinois

HAIR: Brown   EYES: Gray

PERSONALITY: Lively and lovable,
Molly is also patriotic and feisty

YEAR: 1943

Molly and her class knit a blanket to keep soldiers
warm—and they win the school Lend-a-Hand contest!

Molly and her family listen to a radio broadcast while opening Christmas presents.
They hear Dad's voice from the radio, wishing them all a Merry Christmas!

Emily Bennett arrives from war-torn London. She stays with
the McIntire family and makes fast friends with Molly.

LEND-A-HAND

Molly and her friends sew together knitted squares of yarn in many colors to make a blanket to win the Lend-a-Hand contest. Use the grid below to design your own patchwork blanket by using crayons, colored pencils, or markers to color in the squares with whatever design you choose.

NOT IN THIS PICTURE

This picture might look like the same image of Molly and her friends making a blanket, but it's not. Several items are missing. Can you pick out the items that are missing in the scene?

Go back and take a look at the picture on page 57. Stare at it for five seconds to commit it to memory. Then come back to this page to test your memory.

Answers in the back of the book.

MEET MARYELLEN

NAME: Maryellen Larkin

NICKNAME: Ellie

HOME: Daytona Beach, Florida

HAIR: Strawberry Blonde

EYES: Hazel

DREAMS OF: Standing out and being known for her big ideas

YEAR: 1954

Maryellen wants to paint her front door a bright color to make her house
stand out, but she ends up falling in her skates and spilling paint everywhere!

Maryellen joins the Science Club at her school and is excited to invent a flying machine, but the boys in the club just want her to take notes and don't listen to her ideas.

Maryellen has to save her sister Joan, who has fallen off a cliff while searching for their lost dog. She ties a flashlight to the end of a flag so Joan can see in the dark and climb up to safety.

DESIGN A DOOR

Maryellen wanted to make her house stand out from the others on her street, so she painted the door bright red. If you could design your front door any way you'd like, what would you do? Color in the door below any way you'd like.

DOG GONE

Maryellen's beloved dachshund, Scooter, has gone missing. Maryellen and her sister must look for him in the forest. Follow the path below to get him from lost to found.

LOST

FOUND

MEET MELODY

NAME: Melody Ellison

NICKNAME: Dee-Dee

HOME: Detroit, Michigan

HAIR: Dark Brown

EYES: Brown

DREAMS OF: A world in which everyone is treated equally

YEAR: 1964

Melody is thrilled when her brother, Dwayne, asks her to
sing backup as he records his first single at a music studio.

When Melody's older sister Yvonne isn't allowed to apply for a job at
the bank because she is black, Melody protests by closing her account.

Melody and her family listen to Martin Luther King Jr. speak at the Walk to Freedom civil rights march. Melody is inspired by his speech to sing her favorite song at the Youth Day concert.

A SONG IN YOUR HEART

Melody loves to sing and listen to her brother play music.
What are some of your favorite songs? Answer the
questions below. Then write your own song!

What song do you like to
listen to when you're sad?

_____

What is your favorite song that
came out before you were born?

_____

What is your favorite
song to dance to?

_____

What is your all-time
favorite song?

_____

If you could write a song, what
would you want to sing about?
Use the space below to start a song of your own . . .

_____

_____

_____

_____

_____

_____

_____

_____

_____

_____

_____

NOT IN THIS PICTURE

This picture might look like the same image of Melody's recording
session with her brother, but it's not. Several items are missing.
Can you pick out the items that are missing in the scene?

Go back and take a look at the picture on page 69. Stare at it for five seconds
to commit it to memory. Then come back to this page to test your memory.

Answers in the back of the book.

MEET JULIE

NAME: Julie Albright

NICKNAMES: Alley Oop, Jules, and Cool Hands Albright

HOME: San Francisco, California

HAIR: Blonde   **EYES:** Brown

PERSONALITY: Creative, upbeat, and outspoken

YEAR: 1974

Julie and her best friend, Ivy, celebrate Chinese New Year in San Francisco.

Julie loves to play basketball, but she can't join the all-boys team. Julie learns that the Title IX law grants equal rights for girls to play sports in public schools, and she petitions for the right to join the team.

Julie volunteers at a wildlife shelter and organizes a class campaign on
Earth Day to help reintroduce a family of bald eagles to the wild.

FEED THE BIRDS?

Julie uses a puppet to help feed a baby bird that was separated from its mama. Follow the paths below to figure out which one will get the food in the puppet's beak to the baby bird.

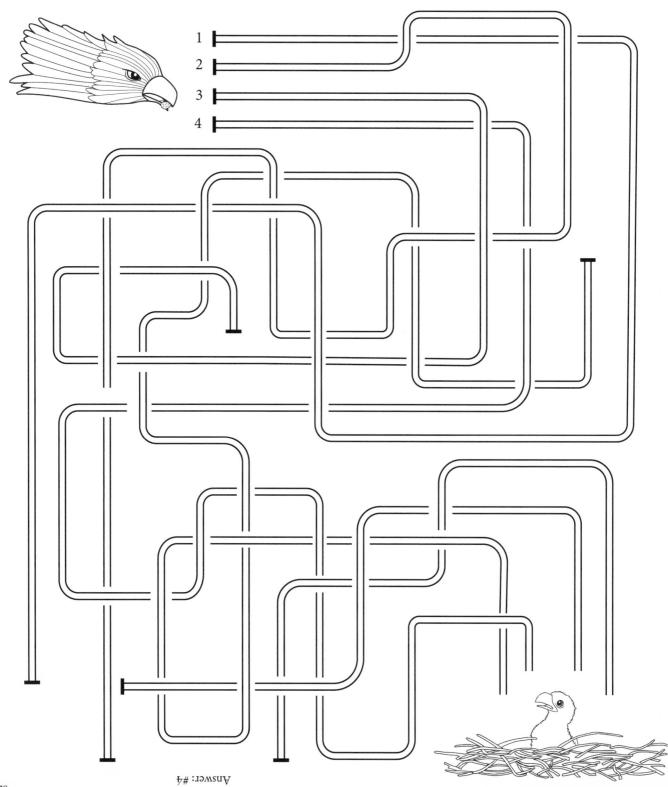

Answer: #4

DECORATING WITH JULIE

Julie is very creative and decorated her room with her mom's help. If you could redecorate your room, how would you change it? Draw it below.

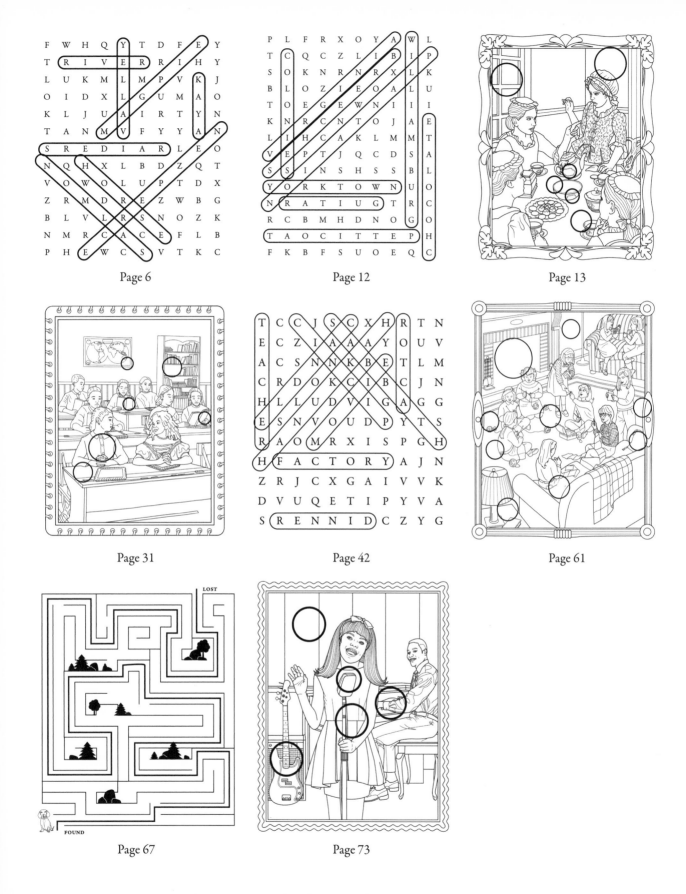

Page 6

Page 12

Page 13

Page 31

Page 42

Page 61

Page 67

Page 73